NIGHT LITE MOTEL:

POEMS, MUSINGS
& SIDEWAYS GLANCES AT THE FILM
INDUSTRY

STEVEN KAUFFMAN

To order additional copies of this book, contact:
Xlibris
844-714-8691
www.Xlibris.com
Orders@Xlibris.com

ISBN: Softcover   978-1-6698-5770-9
       EBook   978-1-6698-5769-3

Print information available on the last page

Rev. date: 11/26/2022

Book and Cover Designed by Douglas Rees
Photo on Back Cover by Deano James

Dedicated to:

Mom; Irish Abie; Tracy, Lanse and Myles, and their families; Tammy; Henri; Bryan; Sondra; David Moe;

AND

family and friends who stood by me through the darkness before there was

a Night Lite.

Table of Contents

Diseased Self, Poet's Soul

Amidst sickness, amidst poverty, humiliation, petulance, grief, Kauffman clings to poetry like a drowning man clings to fantasies of dry land. Sometimes, he must remind himself to breathe. Sometimes, each breath is like swallowing the fetid waters of a polluted sea.

Is Kauffman *the* poet of the diseased times in which we live?

No devilish torture is lacking in his dreadful pandemonium of sickness: migraine headaches, deafening, hammering headaches, which knock him out for days and prostrate him on sofa and bed, abdominal cramps with bloody diarrhea, fevers, lack of appetite, weariness, constipation, chills, night sweats – a gruesome cycle. In addition there are his "all but dead" depressions, which, at the least exertion, overwhelm him with fatigue and grant the poet only two and a half hours of writing a day. But Kauffman despises any yielding to his body and works at his desk for ten hours, and for this excess his overheated brain takes revenge with raging headaches and a nervous overcharge; at night, when the body has long become weary, it does not permit itself to be turned off suddenly, but continues to burrow in visions and ideas until it is forcibly knocked out by drugs. But different drugs are always needed (in two years Kauffman uses up three dozen different preparations to purchase a handful of sleep); then his stomach refuses to pay so high a price and rebels. And now – vicious cycle – spasmodic diarrhea, new headaches which require new medicines, an inexorable, insatiable, passionate conflict of the infuriated organs, which throw the thorny ball of suffering to each other in a mad game. Never a point of rest in this up and down, never an even stretch of contentment or a short month full of comfort and self-forgetfulness. Depressions, fierce as cyclones, bottomless, kidnap him and turn him into a snarling beast, cursing the dog god, cursing the sunlight, cursing love, cursing life.

Among modern writers, perhaps only Nietzche's body rebelled with such brute tyranny against the creative process. Baudelaire likens his poet-self to a "diseased bundle of rags." But it is the Baltimore gutter-poet, Edgar Allen Poe, who amazes Kauffman. In *The Divine Edgar* Kauffman casts his lot with that motley crew of bards and gleemen who have sought to transmogrify the sickness unto death by means of *passionate* suffering.

Oakland's poet laureate, Jack Foley, in his introduction to Kauffman's first published book of poems **Inner View,** stresses the charged, unabashed, decidedly uncool **emotion** of Kauffman's work. Beyond Kauffman's embarrassing earnestness, I am moved by the moral quality of his poetry. That life is unending loss is a given. How to live in full knowledge of that truth is the burning engine driving these poems. How to go on living? *A dash of style/ A little panache* doesn't do it, not when *Death calls.../ With a voice so seductive, so deceptively joyous.../ It is indistinguishable from life.* Life's settled goals, rejected: *The pursuit of happiness, I defy it / An aspiration to greatness, I decry it.*

There is no innocence in Kauffman's world. Awareness begins with awareness of loss – loss of the beloved, loss of health, loss of hope, loss of self. If you are grounded in a sensibility which reports "all is lost, and once lost, lost forever", each and every poem is a forced gesture in search of a way out. Yet, each poem in *Inner View* is an exploration that ends in failure. *Inner View* ends as it begins, with Poe: *And my soul from out that shadow that lies floating on the floor shall be lifted...Nevermore!*

This new book - *Night Lite Motel: Poems, Musings & Sideways Glances at the Film Industry* - coming sixteen years after *Inner View*, does not have the relentless, claustrophobic feel of someone living in a shrinking air bubble. Something has happened; there is room to breathe. The title poem (it's also the lead poem of the volume) seems at first glance to recapitulate the stark themes of *Inner View*. But whereas the emotional tone of that book is dirge-like, *Night Lite Motel* taps out a funky, spunky, bebop/hip hop kool kind of melody, full of word play and comic ambiguity:

> **face the rules   so**
> **chaste the rules we face;**
> **they turn their backs on me**
> **fingers stagger drunkenly across the keyboard /**
> **thoughts inside my**
> **head interpreted through a ouija bored with the words I've**
> **said   often   unwittingly   thoughtful**

Kauffman dissects the ruminating ghosts with sharp wit. "Poet as petitioner" has given way to a writer able to ridicule much of what the culture has idolized, and by doing so, gain power over the old hauntings.

> **If I have an objective in mind,**
> **it is to object to the objects that I objectify.**
> **That is an observation that I find objectionable,**
> **yet many consider it an invisible objectification.**
> **If the object of your affection affects the object**
> **you have in mind, you may have a choice to make.**
> **If so, don't come to me.**

The problem for the writer, for the poet, who is aesthetically, temperamentally, capable of the greatest intensity - or nothing -who is enthralled by romanticism in all senses of the word enthralled, is that the moment of exhilaration does not, cannot last:

> **inspiration has no date**
> **it arrives without a name**
> **it comes when it chooses**
> **and leaves with the changes**
> **slight of thought and hand**

As the last two lines of this stanza recount so beautifully, when the exalted moments go, it is not even possible to identify if the causes lie inside or out. It may be a small, unseemly thought or gesture which kills, or the Muse may take herself away, "now you see me now you don't," with a magical motion that is like death. Romanticism leads to death. What then?

Then one day you walk into a diner and you meet this cutely kooky girl named Tori Amos and she falls in love with you and you can prove it. So there. *Tori Amos Loves Me and I Can Prove It* is a funny piece, refusing to be bitter-sweet, it stands its ground and makes ya laugh. I'd like anyone to show me a piece from the last ten years that is as funny as this one, funny in a human way, unapologetically funny and warm. Suppose this piece were a script, how would I pitch it? Girl meets Bosendorfer, girl loves Bosendorfer. Boy meets girl, boy knows what the fuck a Bosendorfer is, girl loves boy! It's that simple. And the beat goes on. Surprise!

There is much to savor in this new volume. I particularly enjoyed *Sin Jin* whose opening lines

is this performed as it is written?
ah yes, the peacock said.

take their place along side The Master's *Bear in mind / This garden was enchanted!* in the book of magical mystery poems. There is even a short story about art war on the streets of New York which punningly restates the book's title.

Surprises abound in the Night Lite Motel. Just last week I was having a sandwich there. I passed on the one called "Agenbite of Inwit - pickled boar lambasted with stultifying asides." What sounded really good was "Kauffman's Folly - 90% energy and enthusiasm and 10% nubile, naked young women." The menu said the sandwich was invented by the poet, Steven Kauffman, during a drinking binge with Edgar Allen Poe. Poe looked sullen and sipped his absinthe. Kauffman danced on the bar, singing the songs he has been writing, and which you can read...in the *Night Lite Motel*.

Henri Montandon
Walnut Creek
California

NIGHT LITE MOTEL

night lite motel
reservations for pain and tears now accepted
dreams of romance stolen
leaden empty sun swollen, greeting you as
you wake alone
you wake alone
face the rules so
chaste the rules we face;
they turn their backs on me
fingers stagger drunkenly across the keyboard / thoughts
inside my
head interpreted through a ouija bored with the words I've
said often unwittingly thoughtful
in this room remains the remains: the eye (to watch)
                        and I who watch
the window men and women living life
beyond the glass
beyond the pale
unheard the words they say
whilst they don't think
and question which is worse
the proof or lack of it
what good is proof when there's nothing satiable to be?

the ruler of the night / the king
    hiding from the light ...

	alone
iwake	alone
idream	alone
italk	alone
ishare	alone
icry	alone

i's two define the search
to find the search

answers don't come clean   at 500 AM /
the darkness curses me   leave me be
beyond my own devices
devoid of filling the void

sun blinds me with the start of more incrimination / CLOSE THE
BLINDS

and blind me with a lack of social education

it only takes little fingers to blow me away ...
to a head of darkness
miles of vision
indecision
viles of mission
spilt on the floor
unaccomplished
nothing to say
nothing to do
do ... you?
do ... the poet?

is he / could she be
the practicioner or the petitioner?
write it, say it, perform it, live it
as livid and inspired as could be
in search of the wrong discovery
you cannot petition with prayer   and

inspiration has no date
it arrives without a name
it comes when it chooses
and leaves with the changes
slight of thought and hand

        look around and see
huge chaos   in creation
        to provoke society
and transform it
    staring forward
    looking backwards
    through the mirror darkly

a little lucidity would not be amiss

i'd give up my soul for one breathless kiss

OBJECTIVE ELASTICITY

If I have an objective in mind,
it is to object to the objects that I objectify.
That is an observation that I find objectionable,
yet many consider it an invisible objectification.
If the object of your affection affects the object
you have in mind, you may have a choice to make.
If so, don't come to me.
I don't know whether i am I or i am an object.
or i am bic pen   tameter.
I once knew an attorney that i trusted implicitly
And he said "i object!"
Does that answer your question?
or does it provoke you to ask one?
If not, perhaps you can help me answer mine.
That is, if you don't object.

As the following poem's title indicates, I spent most of January, 1991 at Langley / Porter Psychiatric Institute due to a variety of mental and emotional problems. Most prominent among these problems were attacks of rage, uncontrollable anger, and loss of control over my emotions. One of the nurses on duty instructed me that if I should get any warning that I was about to lose control, I should come to her immediately and say "I NEED TO TALK TO YOU!" Shortly after, I started cursing and yelling and realized my anger was building out of control and I went back to the nurse saying "I NEED TO TALK TO YOU! I NEED TO TALK TO YOU!" She took me to my room and said "I'll be back in a few minutes", then closed the door. The following piece describes what then transpired.

JANUARY 1991 AT LANGLEY / PORTER PSYCHIATRIC INSTITUTE

The truth is ...
          that I did the right thing
          that I did what she asked me to do
       and that I told the truth

  but they used words against me
words that said
          I wanted to do the wrong thing
words that said
          I often did the wrong thing
             an even clearer distinction ...
          I was the wrong thing

the lie is ...
          that I admitted urges to harm the others
          I never said that to anyone!
             not to staff
             not to doctors
             not to nurses
             not to patients

but they *documented* that I admitted these urges
and they threw two 5150 forms at me
             at first, 48 hours
             and then,
            as the second 5150 read,
             indefinitely
I told the truth

and
    they told a lie
        and
    I did what I was told to do
        and
    they rewarded that crime with two policemen
    enforcing their rules
        and
    separating the rest of the patients
                        from
    the contagion on two legs that was me
                in their eyes

I said what I felt and
I said it loudly and
though sometimes I might have been out of control
                and
though sometimes I might have been sedated,
I still had an active brain
                and
that made me dangerous to them.

so the cops put the cuffs on my wrists
            and they bled
and the cops dragged me down the hallway
            and
I could see the whole staff and the patients
walking *around* and *beside* my body
                dragging on the floor
            and
I looked up and I asked them
            Why?
What did I do? What was so wrong? Why are you doing this to me?

and I realized ...
there is no need for the truth when there is power
and there is no reason for truth to exist
            when there is autonomy on the inside
            and a powerless outside
and there is no need for a truth called Steven who shoots his mouth off
            and
so easily could upset the apple cart of order

and so they set me up

                            and
they censored me
                            and
they didn't allow me to be what I was.
they censored my thoughts
                            and
they censored my spirit
                            and
they censored me in an isolation tank
                            and
threw me in a padded cell for 24 hours
                            and
I pissed all over me
                            and
I shit all over me
                            because
they refused to unlock the bathroom door
when I pounded with my fists and begged them to
                            and
after 24 hours they opened the door
                            and
said I could try and escape they didn't care
                            and
one hour later they came back and I was still there
                            and
they said all right we'll let you out.

they kept me locked up
                            but
at least I had a bed and a bathroom
                            and
in exchange for that

they censored my words
they censored my brain
they censored my thoughts

so that no one else   none of the others
            remembered me
            cared about me
                            and
I didn't care about myself

I was detached from the world and what some people call reality

and
I could feel nothing but fear and my own pain
and
I howled like a wolf in pain
and they gloated
for they had succinctly and successfully censored me as a person
if it wasn't for the fear and the pain I would be a non-entity
and
if it wasn't for the public defender and the judge at the hearing,
I'd still be lying there today.

and now I'm out on the street
and
supposedly they can't touch me
and
I still tell the truth
and
I do what I think is right
and
I might trust some people
but
I rarely trust anybody I didn't know before I was censored

I'm not a martyr
and
I'm not a hero
and
I'm not a saint

I'm just fucking scared
I'm just fucking scared all the time
I'm always looking behind me and sometimes I see them
ready
with their handcuffs and their weapons
ready
for war to begin anew.

And we *all* better keep looking behind us
Yes we **ALL** better keep looking behind us
because the first or second time when you don't see nothin'
you may be lulled into thinking you don't need to look around a third
and
when you don't look around for the third time
CENSORSHIP PLACES ITS BONY FINGERS AROUND YOUR THROAT
CENSORSHIP PLACES ITS BONY FINGERS AROUND YOUR THROAT

TORI AMOS LOVES ME AND I CAN PROVE IT

It was 15 years ago but it easily could have been yesterday ... the day we first met, that is. She was wearing a psychedelic tie-dyed apron and a waitress uniform that was so low cut, I believe her nipples may have been covered by it, but I doubt it. She had a name tag that said Tori on her left breast. My first thought was, how did she keep from bleeding? Most people bleed when puncturing their skin with metal clothespins.

i'm sultry.
i'm steven, how do you do?
wouldn't you like to know?
is that a rhetorical question or do you think i'd like to know how you do what you do when you do it?
here's the menu, call me when you're ready. until then, i'll be smacking this wad of gum from one side of my mouth to the other.

She started walking away but did an immediate about-face when I uttered the words,
Tori, what do you recommend on the menu?

She said something very stylish that made no sense. When I asked her to repeat it, she said something quite sensual that was not very stylish.

why don't you try the Tori. it's delightful and exciting in appearance but if you try to eat it, that 7', 300 lb. security guard over there named Quasimodo will reach under the table and dismantle your testicles. after 24 hours of refrigeration, you'll find them being served tomorrow as our blue plate special. anything else you need to know?

yes. i have never met you before today. i have not been unkind or insulting to you and unless you're trying out a standup comedy routine on me, i'd like to know what i have done to you that warrants such revolting, disgusting behavior.

you're a man and you haven't made eye contact with me yet; you've only made tit contact and i can do that myself by looking in a mirror. i don't need you for that. now will there be anything else or can i return to my one true love whose name is Bosendorfer and he's sitting in the back.

wait a minute, Tori. you've got a baby grand piano sitting in the back?

you know what a Bosendorfer is? i'm impressed. you may not be as dumb as i thought. you may actually be intelligent and intelligence is dangerous to a slave and i know because i'm a slave ... to my Bosendorfer.

and you're also intelligent.

okay, that's 2 positive impressions you've made on me without so much as using your fingers. so what it'll be, hmm? i don't have all day. i have chords that are waiting to be fingered.

i wouldn't touch that line with a 10 foot pole!!!

(screaming)
you don't have a 10 foot pole!!!!!!!!!!

now that's where you're wrong!
look, i've had just about as much of this non-conversation as i can take.

alright then. here's the deal. you prove to me that you really know how to tickle the ivories of a Bosendorfer as you claim and i'll prove to you that i've got an honest anatomically correct 10 foot pole between my legs. if we both can prove our claims as the absolute truth, you must approach me as a new customer who you've never seen before who just walked in the door and sat down at a table. then you say to me, my name is Tori and i'll be your waitress today. then with a Mona Lisa smile on your lips and your flaming copper hair hanging seductively between our eyes, you treat me with respect and view me as a thoughtful, kind, intelligent man and not some roadkill you just took great pleasure in demolishing. will you accept those terms and do we have a deal?

yes, by all means. i would consider your having a 10 foot pole a very strong argument for treating you with respect and kindness, maybe even love.

great. shall we adjourn to the back room?

you better let me go first. you might have a little trouble maneuvering your ... pole.

Swiveling onto her piano stool, she positioned her fingers on the keyboard, then glanced up at me with a warm smile that quickly froze into petrified meanness.

this is called THE WAITRESS. start counting. i'll give you about 2½ minutes of it.

As she finished, she looked up at me with a genuine unpretentious smile on her face.

since you've been such a marvelous audience and now that you see i'm not - made of bullshit, i'll give you a bonus (not that you deserve it).
this is CORNFLAKE GIRL.

I stood there dumbfounded speechless lost on her magical path of speed and brilliance.

i'm utterly astounded. you're not only a magnificent musician, but i've never heard such a unique vocal style.
nobody sings like that. nobody. Only Tori.
i think i like you Tori. maybe i even love you.

enough of the bullshit, although i do honestly appreciate your complements. but don't say LOVE to me. don't EVER say LOVE to me. i don't want to hear a bullshit man try to bullshit his way into my body proclaiming bullshit love. now i've shown you mine. let's see yours now or don't waste another second of my time.

i made a promise and i live up to my promises.

With my jeans down below my knees, I looked into her eyes for a response. I couldn't tell whether it was her eyes or her mouth that were opened wider with shock and awe. She tried to talk but couldn't. Finally her Mona Lisa smile returned.

you sure it's ONLY 10 feet?

I pulled up my jeans very slowly watching the enjoyment in her eyes as she followed the long, long reassertion take place.

okay, you win. would you mind leaving and coming back through the front door in about two minutes?

you're not gonna go back on your word, are you?

i wouldn't lie to a man that i love.

love?

yes love. i learned a very important lesson from you just now. i want to be a woman who loves and respects a man for what he is and for what i am. i don't care if you were 2" at your hardest. i feel something real for you and even if it lasts no longer than one minute, i wanted you to know it. i love you. now get out of here and walk in the front door in two minutes. got that?

got it.

good. i'll be waiting for you.

We never saw each other again after that afternoon at the Dew Drop Inn. She went on to have an illustrious career and make a lot of money. I went on to Oakland, CA where i spent the summers watching ants crawl across my kitchen cabinets. But whenever i listen to one of her cds or watch her provocatively swivel and slide on her piano stool during a TV appearance or a video, i never forget that, 15 years ago, Tori Amos loved me and i can prove it.

THERE'S A LIFE INSIDE YOU

There's a life inside you.
sometimes when you search hard and deep
                                you discover it
the winning gamepiece on the inner lid on a container
                        of yogurt.
2 yogurts a day everyday for more than 6 weeks and finally,
the gamepiece you've needed all this time comes up and
                                to your surprise,
                you've won the prize!
a Dannon a day for a year ... for free!

There's a life inside you.
and it speaks to you in fluid English,
                eloquent French,
                fluent Spanish,
                and Apocryphalese,
                                isn't that joyful?
as you push your Safeway shopping cart filled with all of your
                                meager belongings
down the same full / empty streets
with the same depressed / confused / enigmatic thoughts
accompanying the same parade of
                denigrating / desolating / derisive faces
laughing at anything, everything, each other
                                and maybe ... you.

There's a life inside you.
and sometimes when you try to find it
                try to uncover and
                try to review it,
                it's not there.
don't savage the shovel in continuous search
digging through crusty crags of mothballs cobwebs and
                                fake fur-less phantasm
life will appear as an exclamation,
                not as an excavation!

11

There's a life inside you.
though you may have forgotten it's there <u>and</u>
it shows up in the strangest places
wearing a formal tuxedo and tales
                              and informal sneakers
                              purple and blue
                              with terse teal laces.
sit in the dark and watch their faces
ten foot tall in body size,
their thoughts ... their dreams
are they as small and compact as mine?
look at him   as he caresses her face
softly sweetly   tenderly touches
her lustrous red hair   or is it
                        purple or blue
                        with terse teal cornrows?
find comfort in the darkness.   you're alone
and no one can see you
only you can see them
and the parts they choose to show
as you witness   eternal sunshine
the only constant miraculous bath of light

                                        in your spotless mind
you watch it again   and again   and again
until you can no longer sit in the darkness
bathing in light that is ten foot tall,   cause ...
they're cleaning the last lost kernels of buttery popcorn and
              melted candy bars and
              spilled sticky soda
clinging to your   informal sneakers.
          cannot breathe
          cannot stand
          cannot leave,   cause ...
she didn't look at you   and caress your face
softly sweetly   tenderly touching
your lustrous blond hair   or is it
                        purple or blue
                        with terse teal baldness concealed.
a pounding heart was created for both of them to share, but you
weren't included

                              as part of that deal

when you paid your admission and got your ticket stub
and when you're forced
                              to leave the soothing darkness   and
blind your burning eyes with taut truthful light,
                    she has gone
                    he has gone
to that ten foot tall life that exists only in darkness
where you find life inside you existing in darkness
and wait to discover it alight   in the light
and wait ... and wait ...
and write ... and write ...
and find ...

There's a life inside you.
PULL IT OUT!
LIVE IT!

THE JEFFREY LEVY-HINTE STORY

Jeffrey Levy-Hinte was a New York artsy guy who came from a family of big-time money, and also was getting a lot of financial backing from other New York artsy wannabes. He had only one associate working with him - a fat, dumb, Asian-American guy who was constantly causing him grief because of the guy's stupidity.

Jeffrey loved the documentary film FROM HOLLYWOOD TO HANOI but after meeting the director, Tiana, he despised her. She was trying to get money out of him and was playing up to him, but she told me personally that she thought he was even dumber than his associate and was a talentless shithead who would never amount to anything. Then she told somebody else the same thing about Jeffrey, but that other person went right back to Jeffrey with her comments. Because Jeffrey knew how good I was in the business and had heard that other big-name people had great respect for my abilities, (word spreads quickly in the NYC entertainment scene), he made an offer to me to join him in forming a film production company. He said he had so much money behind him that he could pay me well and we would make a lot of money together. (Considering that Tiana wasn't paying me at all, any offer he made would have been paying me well).

I became the man in the middle between them. I clearly remember a day in which Tiana and I had a meeting with Jeffrey at the warehouse / loft building that he owned in Soho or Tribeca. What started out as a cordial discussion, rapidly degenerated into a cursing, screaming nasty war between the two of them. Suddenly, I felt Tiana's hand reaching under my shirt and down my back till she reached my belt. Within seconds, she was dragging me out the door by my belt, while the two of them were cursing and screaming epithets at one another with me stuck in the middle between them. I wouldn't have minded if her hand down my back and her death grip on my belt was the start of some kind of sexual encounter between us. But in this case, she was just tearing me away from him (literally) before he could professionally tear me away from her. However, this battle wasn't over yet. Something that Tiana screamed at him really set Jeffrey off; and he threw a punch at her face. It never connected with her because it glanced off the side of my head instead.

Jeffrey felt terrible about punching me by mistake and started apologizing stating he was aiming for THE BITCH and didn't mean ... and that's as far as his apology got, because Tiana, noticing that he was looking directly at me & had temporarily forgotten her, seized the opportunity and landed a haymaker to his jaw. Jeffrey was a big man, bigger than Tiana and me combined. But the force of him flying against the wall after her punch was so powerful that I knew Tiana had really nailed him. Next thing I knew, she and I were out on the sidewalk but my jeans were almost down to my knees because during the struggle, Tiana had pulled my belt off & ripped the button off the top of my jeans. She was the only one who came out of it without an injury or mishap of any kind. After finding my belt on the ground and re-fastening my pants, I heard Tiana yelling "Oh shit! Help me, Steve! He's coming after me! Help me, Steve!" And she started running down the street like a bat out of hell. My head was still buzzing from Jeffrey's inadvertent punch, and I didn't want to stand around and find out what an accurate punch from him felt like. So I raced after Tiana till we got to the end of the block. I turned around to see how close he was, only to discover that he was still standing in the doorway of the building with his face covered with blood.

During our half-cab, half-walk back to the office, Tiana kept hugging and kissing me, alternating between apologizing for my getting hit and thanking me for "rescuing her". When we got back to our office in the Du-Art building, she wasted no time in taking off her clothes to show me how much she appreciated my "rescue" efforts.

A couple days later, she was off to Toronto with a print of the film for the Toronto Film Festival. That afternoon, I got a call at the office from Jeffrey. He was extremely apologetic saying that he didn't care what happened to Tiana but he was very upset about me being caught up in the middle of their personal feud and about hitting me with a punch that was meant for her. After a couple minutes, we began to talk about the business. He told me about a project he was working on. He had done a first draft adaptation of an Anton Chekhov story that he updated to modern day New York City and was sure he could get a big-name actress to play the lead. But he wanted and needed me to work with him on it He also said that under no circumstances would he ever have anything more to do with the "Yellow Fever Bitch", a name he was calling her to her face two days before. He got into a rant about how Tiana was a 2 or 3 or 4 faced bitch who would go about manipulating any man she needed to advance her career by playing the part of a sweet, earnest, hardworking put-upon struggling filmmaker and by shoving her big fat tits in their face. He wanted me to walk out on her and start working with him on the film project he had given the name UPHEAVAL. But timing and fate worked against that happening, even if I had wanted it to.

By the end of the following week, FROM HOLLYWOOD TO HANOI was booked into the Film Forum in NYC, and I was getting phone calls from Richard Corliss at Time Magazine and the film critic from Playboy Magazine, Bruce Williamson saying that in addition to reviewing FROM HOLLYWOOD TO HANOI, they both wanted to write feature articles about Tiana and "the new Asian cinema". And could I please send them stills from the film to accompany the articles. And would I make arrangements for an interview with her as soon as possible because each one wanted to be the first national film critic to do a major article on her. Things continued to explode from that point on and I never had the opportunity to go any further with the Jeffrey Levy-Hinte UPHEAVAL film project, and never ran into or talked to him again.

On Christmas Eve 2004, I watched a 1977 horror film that I've always enjoyed a lot called SUSPIRIA which was being shown on the Independent Film Channel. And right after it finished, a movie came on called (you guessed it) UPHEAVAL. Produced and adapted from Chekhov by Jeffrey Levy-Hinte and starring Frances McDormand, who made this film just before winning the Best Actress Oscar for her performance in the Coen Brothers' film FARGO.

CONCEPTUAL ROMANTICISM

I've been thinking about concepts like art and beauty, laughter and pain, and the purpose of our existence. Mostly my thoughts keep returning to the word "love".

I recalled a 25 year old black woman named Rhonda and I wondered ... is it possible that at an age of such youth and innocence, one could truly have, as Elvis Costello put it, "a suitcase of wisdom to dispense" and to carry with you. A suitcase that even at that tender age was so packed with intelligence, joy, peace and contentment that there was no room left inside for the prejudice and injustice in the world the suitcase and its owner must travel through. Ah. but there was just enough room left in that bag for one other thing ... pure unadulterated love.

I've been wondering if something like that could honestly, truthfully be possible. I've struggled with that thought for a very long time. Finally I walked away from it thinking "Who knows what is possible ... and what isn't?"

But if possible does exist, and if love does exist, why can't we the human inhabitants of this planet love life and live love. Is it shameful or a sign of weakness to live love as a statement of beauty and art? If love is omnipresent, don't we share it with the omnipotent and with one another? Isn't it completely realistic to live a life of love inside the words of a heartfelt deeply romantic poem? And within that sweet context, love does exist.

2 RAINDROPS AND THE SUN (FOR MY MOTHER)

The clouds contain a hint of rain
Small groups of people meet
To lionize and sterilize
The earth beneath their feet

The wounds that blind midst souls that bind
Ascend through naked air
Then dissipate and can't negate
The love now resting there

One life alone, unique, her own
Projected on our screens
For all to see, aspire to be
Restored within our dreams

Her gifts to me, her artistry,
"I'll be seeing you anon"
Like a vivid, vibrant canvas
Of 2 raindrops and the sun.

THINK... BELIEVE

What I think and what I believe are two different things.

What I believe runs far deeper than what I think.

I think that I'm a pretty intelligent guy and a good person.
I think I'm a caring, thoughtful, sensitive & sincere individual.
I think I'm a multi-talented artist.
I think there's nothing wrong with me.

BUT...

I believe that I'm a small, weak, sick insignificant jerk.
I believe that there is not a woman in this world that ever could possibly be interested in me unless she was
more of a creep than I am.
I believe that most other people choose to ignore me or pretend that I don't exist
I believe that no one has any respect for me, least of all myself.
I believe that there is no such thing as happiness allowed in my life, nor will there ever be.
I believe that I am more of a monster than the computer BEAST itself.

Since I BELIEVE all this horrible stuff about myself to be true, what does it matter what I THINK?

For everyone who has ever experienced sweet, tender and joyful romantic love ...

MY FAVORITE THEME IS YOU

would it matter to you if my eyes were green or hazel or brown or blue?
could the words i softly whispered to you be believed cause they were true,
if your skin was white or black or brown or a shade invented just for you
if the words you said were truly meant and not puppets of indifference, untrue.

do you care how old the universe is?
does it matter how long I've existed?
do you think false words that others state should be believed / inspired / insisted
or to waste your youth and love on me should, at all costs, be resisted.

there is no explanation or rational cause for indifference,
there is but one most magical musical purpose for existence.

whether life takes form within without below

                                    inside the soul
                                    or the heart
                                            or far

above,
there is music that only you can play
and it lives in the soul of your love.

SPARE PARTS

walking through these rooms

is not an easy flight

catacombs and tombs

on a dark and dirty night

falling up through turban clouds

not breathing in the air

should you want a piece of me

i have a heart to spare

BASEBALL

Life is the pitcher. I am the batter. The pitcher keeps throwing at my head. I keep hitting the dirt, but many times I can't get out of the way of the pitch. But I must continue to shake off the pain, dust myself off and get back in the batter's box ready for the next pitch. If I don't do that, I'll never hit one out of the park once in awhile. That's what it's all about. Being a hero in my own eyes.

THE AFTER - DEATH

a fierce cold wind battered my heart and left me empty and naked
ensconced in darkness
i traversed a swirling path of razor edged emeralds ablaze with
translucent moonbeams firing off sparks of passion in every direction
but i couldn't feel them
for i had no feet

i entered a teardrop and felt the cold / hot wetness saturate me,
envelope me and carry me back into the blue green origin of sight

i slid down a waterfall of burgundy and balsam
reaching out for a soul to cling to and avoid being swept further away
but found no island to contain me. no sinew to restrain me
and floated in white hot darkness
suddenly parted by an eternal light and though i had no eyes to see,
a vision of god appeared on a throne and i reached out to him and
basked in the glory surrounding his face
and he appeared to be a reflection of me ... with no eyes

reached out to touch the tip of his beard
but it slipped through fingers i no longer had
descentment transcended resentment as i slid ever deeper
toward where i had begun

the kernel of me continued to be
as it touched on a surface of soft, sweet and silky waves and the
balm of a woman i might have once known

i felt joy in her face and warmth in her smile
as she shuddered and quivered ecstatically
and tasted her neck, her alabaster shoulder,
then dripped to the heat of perfection ...
her breast
with pink brownish nipple pointing up toward the heavens
i suckled with passion lost for centuries
and the milk that i drew enriched by her soul
restored and enlivened my spirit anew
and i became what i was meant to be ...

                                        again

SIN JIN

is this performed as it is written?
ah yes, the peacock said.
"died?" i inquired.
"at the top of his form?"
that wan whose tail i toll
when i questioned COLLABORATION
we lay sheik to sheik
begob it's the Charles Bukowski writealike contest
shure it's the plithery
                        plathery
and mine funned me just a mome's meant ago
are you sure we're up and Adam?

verbilious ruckmaking
glimmerglam shivvershoes on her swayways
can we never seas the day
or the seasoning
have we flayed the peacock once again?
sickles they are. one after thea otter

HOW TO CHANGE YOUR LIFE (WITH A GREAT FILM)

During a period of five months. I experienced the sudden demise of an intensely passionate and deeply loving relationship, followed by the unexpected and torturous illness and death of my Mother, and then was nearly killed myself in an horrendous car accident. These experiences, coming on the heels of one another, left me questioning LOVE, LIFE, DEATH and my own mortality.

Why do we choose to share our lives, experiences and memories with others when the odds aren't necessarily in favor of a positive outcome? WHY DO WE LOVE?

Michel Gondry & Charlie Kaufman's multi-layered, multi-textured ETERNAL SUNSHINE OF THE SPOTLESS MIND addressed these issues in a cinematic mirror image of real people in real life situations. The film surprised and inspired me because it provided some clues, some answers. And it touched nerves. One of the most challenging, romantic and poetic movies ever made, it featured career performances from Jim Carrey & Kate Winslet. I walked into ETERNAL SUNSHINE feeling empty and thirsting for hope. I walked out of it filled with INTERNAL SUNSHINE.

LIFE CYCLE

while udders explain
the moo sickle al dente
eat
          drink
                    sleep
                              fuck
                                        piss
                                                shit

die
erection diverse
tick u loquacious dockers

hebrew goddess mem bare rain / run rabbit updyke from /
penisless whoopie cushions
eat
          drink
                    sleep
                              fuck
                                        piss
                                                shit

die

up stickies forum multi bloody vistas, man /
icey dicey wombat conjugating verb - o - grams /
her essay religion / stupid ass republic /
casting doubt with jailbait / on its access hookey /
existential nipples hidden in a bottle /
aroma desperately seeking cleavage for friendship /
(or for marriage) /
heat seeking missile for audacious want
ads / subtracts desire equation
head less whores squeeze pimple / white
release long lawn laun / dree list lazy lousy
lump of coal inside your stocking /
second cities seconds infiltrate second story / men
filtering hiccuping banana boats

day o day - ay - ay - o

in condescend femmes form fabric coated factsheets /
illustrated history alliteration fat farm /
empty poets hiding 40's universal /
horror reticent roman nations remem bare room
at the top where /
gossamer gossipminded sirens scream on
an   ambitious   ambulance   to   hell

an   ambitious   ambulance   to   hell

KAUFFMAN'S FOLLY

Personally, I think the wisdom and cunning triumph of old age is overrated. I'll take youth, energy and enthusiasm for 90% of my life, and nubile naked young women for the other 10%.

Printed in the United States
by Baker & Taylor Publisher Services